I Want an Apple
How My Body Works

by DAVID L. HARRISON   Illustrated by DAVID CATROW

HOLIDAY HOUSE   NEW YORK

To Annie Busch, dear friend and visionary leader,
who cares about things that matter

—D.L.H.

To River, I know you don't like apples,
but you love your flying Kong

—D.C.

The publisher thanks Michael Traister, MD, for his expert review of this book.

Printed and bound in June 2021 at C&C Offset, Shenzhen, China.

The artwork was created with pencils, watercolors, and inks.

www.holidayhouse.com

First Edition

1 3 5 7 9 10 8 6 4 2

Library of Congress Cataloging-in-Publication Data is available

ISBN: 978-0-8234-4104-4 (hardcover)

Thank you, apple,
for feeding my body
and helping me stay
smart, healthy, and strong.

I want an apple.

Smart brain,

help me find one.

Sturdy feet, help me stand.

Long legs, help me walk.

Happy heart—
thumpity-thump—
keep me strong so I
can hunt for an apple.

Sniffy nose,

smell the apple.

Bright eyes, help me see it.

Strong arms,
reach across
the table.

Nimble fingers,

pick it up.

Clever hands,
touch the apple.

Sharp teeth,
bite the apple.

Open ears,
hear it crunch.

Busy tongue,
taste the apple.

Yum!

Bye-bye, apple.

All gone.

23

Rumbly tummy,
break it
into tiny pieces.

24

Intestines,
keep what I need
and throw away the rest.

27

I love my heart—
thumpity-thump.

29

I love my body—

busy, busy.

I love me.